The story of
RADIO
by F. G. GOODALL
with illustrations by ROBERT AYTON

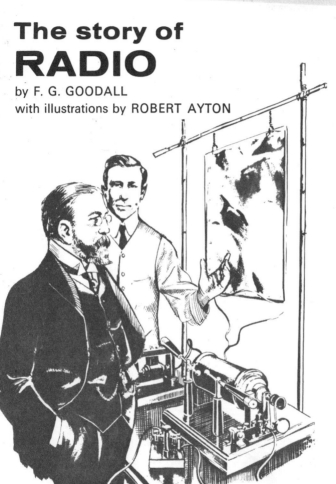

Publishers: Ladybird Books Ltd . Loughborough
© Ladybird Books Ltd (formerly Wills & Hepworth Ltd) 1968
Printed in England

Before radio was invented

Men have always wished to send information over long distances. To do this they shouted across valleys, made smoke signals like the Red Indians did, lighted beacons to warn England of the approaching Spanish Armada, hoisted flag signals, used the sun's light and a mirror – the heliograph, used their arms to wave semaphore signals, 'blinked' messages by Morse lamp, passed word from man to man in a human chain, or beat drums in jungles.

Sometimes such signals could not be made, and at the best they had a limited range. On a sunless day the heliograph was useless, wind sometimes dispersed smoke signals, a man's voice could be heard only over short distances, semaphore and a Morse lamp were read only across the distance they could be seen, and human chains broke down over difficult country.

Then the telephone and telegraph were invented and cables laid on ocean beds to link continents, but these were not always satisfactory; earthquakes, hurricanes, fires and floods often put these means of communication out of action. They were also very costly to install and maintain.

Ships at sea were cut off from all news unless they chanced to pass close to other ships.

Increasing world populations and trade put an even greater strain on existing means of communication. Something had to be done to relieve this strain.

A torpedo boat and flagship of the first World War exchange messages by semaphore

7214 0226 7

How radio began

The story of radio began when, as long ago as 1864, a Cambridge University professor, James Clerk Maxwell, completed an amazing work of pure mathematics that dealt with something with which he had never worked – the stresses and strains in space we now know as 'radio waves'.

Maxwell foretold many of the laws which govern these waves. He said they travelled at 186,000 miles (300,000,000 metres) a second, and that in the same manner as light waves they could be bent, absorbed, reflected and focused. He added that although light waves illuminate an object, radio waves would not do this, but would change the nature of the object on which they were focused.

Scientists everywhere coldly received Maxwell's prophecies, and even the great Lord Kelvin did not believe that he was right. Unfortunately Maxwell died before his theories were proved to be correct.

In the year 1879, a man called Edward Hughes, using a receiver he himself had made, listened in the heart of London to those very radio waves Maxwell had told about, but like Maxwell, Hughes was not believed. Even that great scientific authority, the Royal Society, did not believe him.

Heinrich Hertz proves Maxwell was right

Eight more years passed before a German, Heinrich Hertz, made an experiment which proved Maxwell had been right.

Hertz used simple apparatus – just two Leyden jars. A Leyden jar is a type of 'condenser' (something which can store up an electrical charge), and is made by coating with metal foil the outside and inside of a glass jar.

Hertz put a Leyden jar on one side of a room, and a second jar on the opposite side of the room. Each jar had a small spark-gap connected across its metal coatings.

Now came one of the greatest moments in the history of radio. When Hertz electrically charged one jar, a spark jumped across its spark-gap. Almost instantly a spark crackled across the spark-gap of the other jar. Radio waves had been created by the discharge of the first Leyden jar, crossed the room at 186,000 miles a second and had *induced*, that is *forced*, into the other jar an electrical charge that made it spark.

This proved that radio waves existed and could be transmitted without wires across space. These waves became known as 'Hertzian waves' after the German, Hertz.

Professor Maxwell's calculations had been proved to be absolutely correct.

Heinrich Hertz proves that radio waves could be created

When given a high voltage charge, Leyden jar 'A' sparked

Radio waves from jar 'A' induced an electrical charge in jar 'B' causing it to spark

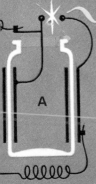 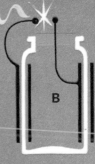

What is wave motion?

If we study waves on water, it will help us to under-stand radio waves, always remembering that radio waves travel at 186,000 miles a second in ether (something which is supposed to be in everything – wood, glass, mountains, sea, air, etc.).

On a calm day, stand on the bank of a pond and throw a fair-sized stone so that it plunges into the pond near the centre. From the point where the stone hits the water, rings of ripples will spread out towards the banks of the pond. If you put a cork or toy boat onto the water, it will bob up and down when the ripples – or small waves – reach it.

When you listen to a radio transmission such as a Morse-code message or a BBC programme, the trans-mitting aerial at the BBC is giving 'punches' to the ether, just like your stone did to the water in the pond. Rings of radio waves spread out from the transmitting aerial, and, when they pass across the aerial attached to your receiver, they induce (remember this word), or *force*, electrical currents to flow up and down in it, and you hear Morse-code signals, the human voice or music. Your receiver may be likened to the cork or boat which bobbed up and down in the pond.

HOW TO MEASURE THE LENGTH OF A WAVE

normal water level

wave length can be measured from any point on the
wave to a similar point further on — for example
om 'A' to 'A', 'B' to 'B', or 'C' to 'C'.

How radio waves were turned into readable signals

After Hertz sent radio waves across a room, nobody did very much about it until, in 1894, Oliver Lodge (later Sir Oliver Lodge) transmitted radio waves a distance of 150 yards.

Hertz had seen that the radio waves created by the spark on his first Leyden jar had induced a spark across the spark-gap of the second Leyden jar, but radio waves from an electric spark can only cause a click to be heard in headphones or through a loudspeaker. You hear this happen when someone switches off a light-switch near your radio. Sir Oliver Lodge realised that if radio waves were to produce a readable message, a further step had to be taken.

The next step was the invention of the 'coherer'. This was a small glass tube, loosely packed with iron filings which did not easily pass current from a battery connected to the tube. However, if an aerial having radio frequency currents flowing in it was connected to a coherer, then the iron filings 'cohered' or stuck more closely together and allowed the current from the battery to flow easily through them, and so ring a bell. Therefore, each time the transmitting aerial radiated waves into the ether, and induced radio currents into a receiving aerial, direct current passed from the battery through the coherer, and rang the bell.

By using a Morse Key at the transmitter, messages were sent out and made readable at the receiver by the coherer.

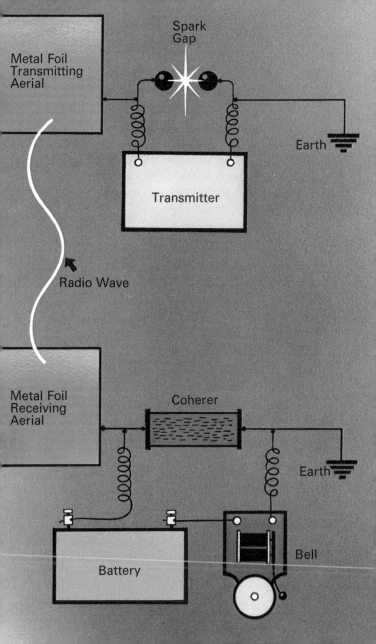

A look backwards in the story of radio

It was in 1884, almost ten years before Lodge transmitted radio waves 150 yards, that William Preece (engineer-in-chief to the British Post Office), noticed some strange signals in overhead telegraph wires in London. He traced the cause of these mysterious signals to currents flowing in some underground cables. The overhead telegraph wires were eighty feet above the ground in which the cables were buried. Such an effect is know as 'induction'.

Let us examine this induction a little more closely. If an electric current flows in a wire, around that wire will spread out magnetic lines of force called a 'magnetic field'. You cannot see this 'field', but it can be shown to be there by holding a small magnetic compass close to the wire. The compass needle swings about when the current is switched on or off.

If a second wire is within the field of the first wire, then into the second wire will be 'induced', that is to say *forced*, the same sort of current as is flowing in the first wire.

William Preece thought that if the underground cables could, by accident, induce signals into the overhead telegraph wires, then signals from one set of previously arranged wires could be induced into another set of wires many miles away. He hoped by this means to transmit signals over long distances without any connecting wires.

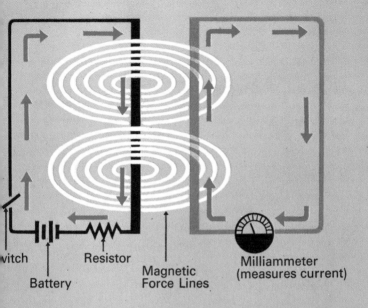

| witch | Battery | Resistor | Magnetic Force Lines | Milliammeter (measures current) |

a magnetic field from one wire cuts across another wire,
to the second wire will be induced — that is, forced — a
rrent similar to that in the first wire, <u>but only when</u>
<u>e current in the first wire (and therefore the magnetic</u>
<u>ld around it) is changing</u>. It could be changed by
arting and stopping the current in the first wire by a
vitch, or sending through it 'alternating current' — which
gularly rises and falls like the waves on the pond.

eneral idea of inductive system of transmitting
essages. Aerial 'A' had current fed into it. It was
ped that the magnetic field around 'A' would
duce signals into aerial 'B' but the idea proved
npracticable over long distances.

An early experiment fails

One Sunday night in the year 1896, William Preece arranged for telegraph lines throughout the length of England to be connected up, and for the same to be done with the telegraph lines in Ireland. His idea was that electric currents in the wires in England might induce similar currents in the Irish wires. However, no definite messages could be successfully passed between the two countries.

Preece (who was later knighted) was keenly interested in radio, knew a great deal about radio waves and did much to develop radio for the Post Office. He was a Fellow of the Royal Society and soon realised that his beliefs in an 'inductive system' were not justified by the facts, and that such a system could not achieve what he had earlier believed possible when he wrote a paper about 'The possibility of sending radio signals through space'.

Other experimenters, using such an *inductive* system, succeeded in passing messages across a quarter of a mile, but the length of wire used in both the transmitter and the receiver, had to be equal to the distance messages had to be sent. Thus, to send a message, say fifty miles, two lots of wire each fifty miles long, had to be erected parallel to each other, and fifty miles apart. The idea was unworkable.

Victorian scientists debate the various radio theories of their time

The amazing Marconi

Any plans the British Post Office may have had for developing Preece's 'inductive system' were dropped when Preece received a letter in the year 1896, introducing him to a young Italian, Guglielmo Marconi, who made what seemed to be astounding claims for his system of *wireless telegraphy*.

Marconi admitted he used apparatus which other experimenters had used – a high voltage spark-coil, a coherer, and so on – but he brought with him to England, amongst other apparatus, a mysterious black box and some sort of electrical relay.

What Marconi *did* claim to have discovered was that the longer he made the aerial 'arms' of his Hertz apparatus, the greater the distance the radio waves covered. He then went on to say that, after many experiments, he had found that if he raised one 'arm' of his aerial, and buried the other 'arm' – earthed it – in the ground, he could send radio waves several miles instead of only a few yards.

Young Marconi had discovered the tremendous importance of an aerial-earth system, and so made radio transmissions over great distances a real possibility.

The young Marconi shows his apparatus to William Preece

Marconi's successful demonstrations

William Preece asked Marconi to give demonstrations of his system. This Marconi did on the roof of the General Post Office, London and again on Salisbury Plain over a distance of one and a half miles. High-ranking military officers were present, and were greatly impressed with what Marconi showed them.

Preece told young Marconi that the British Post Office would spare no expense in backing his experiments. On May 17th, 1897, Marconi made trial transmissions from Lavernock Point, on the coast of Glamorganshire, to Flat Holm Island. The distance was eight miles. On May 18th he successfully sent radio signals from Lavernock Point to Brean Down, Somerset. During these trials a very interesting fact was discovered: radio communication was much easier over water than across land!

Preece did all he could to persuade the Government to back Marconi financially, but there were troubles in South Africa and also at home, so the money was refused.

Marconi went back to Italy. This was a severe blow to William Preece, as he had hoped to keep Marconi working with the British Post Office researchers.

Marconi transmits across
water to Flat Holm Island

Experiments continue and
Marconi returns to England

Although Marconi went back to Italy, experiments went on in England. A Post Office official set up radio apparatus at Bath, and successfully received signals from a transmitter on Salisbury Plain, thirty-four miles away.

Then Marconi returned to Britain – at that time the greatest maritime power in the world and to whom the possibilities of radio contact between ships were of tremendous potential importance.

A Marconi station was set up at Alum Bay, Isle of Wight, and this kept in touch with a radio-equipped vessel cruising near Swanage, Poole Bay and Bournemouth. Constant communication was maintained over a range of eighteen miles.

Other experimental stations were installed at Bournemouth and Poole Bay, where Marconi carried out many tests. This was in the year 1898, and Poole Bay radio station closed down only as recently as 1926.

Marconi also experimented on board Italian warships, and sent messages between them across a distance of twelve miles.

Although the British Government did not back Marconi, other people were willing to do so. He was offered £15,000 and a half share in a company to promote his work and inventions.

The range of the Alum Bay radio transmitter

THAMPTON WATER

SPITHEAD

ISLE OF WIGHT

SOLENT

ALUM BAY

18 MILES

Lloyd's of London become interested

It was in the year 1898 that the world-famous insurance corporation, Lloyd's of London, became interested in what Marconi was doing and asked him to demonstrate his system.

Marconi chose Ballycastle in north-eastern Ireland, and Rathlin Island off that coast, to carry out his tests. These tests were successful. It is true that the distance was only seven and a half miles, but the terrain was not favourable for the transmission and reception of radio waves, being mostly over land and with a high cliff and very little water between the transmitting and receiving stations.

In the same year as the Ballycastle tests, Marconi fitted the steamer *Flying Huntress* with his apparatus, and also set up a receiving station at the house of the harbour master at Kingston, Ireland. The Kingston Regatta was being held at the time, and results of the various events were radioed from *Flying Huntress* to the harbour master's house.

In December 1898, Marconi sent signals from the South Foreland lighthouse to the East Goodwin lightship, a distance of twelve miles. For two years this radio link between lighthouse and lightship was maintained, and, because of it, several ships were prevented from sinking and a number of lives saved. Radio had commenced to *save life and property*.

The successful radio link between lighthouse and lightship

The English Channel spanned by radio

The year 1899 saw radio becoming of world-wide interest. In the summer of that year, the British Association held a meeting in Dover at which the famous scientist, Dr. J. A. Fleming, lectured.

During the lecture George Kempe of the British Post Office sent a long radio message of congratulation to the French Association which was meeting at Boulogne.

The message was transmitted from Dover to the French radio station at Wimereux, and then by land-line to Boulogne. The French Association replied to the British message through Wimereux radio station and Dover. The English Channel had been spanned by radio! The scientific world was keenly interested in this achievement, and the newspapers were excited about it.

In the same year – 1899 – the British Royal Navy became more interested in radio and, using Marconi's system, three Royal Navy warships on manoeuvres kept continuously in touch with one another over a distance of 74 miles.

That year, the United States Navy began fitting radio in its ships, and the progress of the yachts *Shamrock* and *Columbia* in American waters was reported by radio.

In 1901 the German Norddeutscher Lloyd Company fitted radio on its vessels, and ss. *Lake Champlain* became the first British merchant ship to be equipped with radio.

Diagram of an early Marconi transmitter, and a warship of 1899

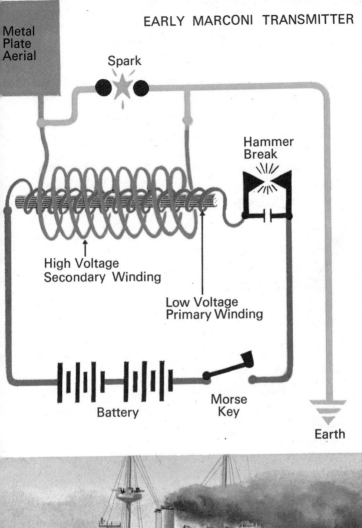

EARLY MARCONI TRANSMITTER

Metal Plate Aerial

Spark

Hammer Break

High Voltage Secondary Winding

Low Voltage Primary Winding

Battery

Morse Key

Earth

Radio signals span the Atlantic Ocean

A radio station was installed at Poldhu in Cornwall, and on December 12th 1901, Marconi himself received at St. John's, Newfoundland, radio messages sent from Poldhu, 2,170 miles away. The Atlantic Ocean had now been spanned by radio!

What a tremendous advance this was from the calculations and theories of James Clerk Maxwell, and the sending by Hertz of radio waves across a room.

The Marconi Company then put up radio stations around the British coasts at Crookhaven, Malin Head, Rosslare, Withernsea, Caister, The Lizard, Inistrahull, Niton and North Foreland. Stations were also installed at Belle Isle, Canada; Chateau Bay, Canada; Sagaponack, U.S.A., and Borkum in Germany.

Very soon the Marconi Company was operating world-wide radio services and handling 6,800 messages a year. Poldhu radio station commenced sending-out daily radio news-bulletins in Morse code, and these quickly became a very popular feature of shipboard life.

Marconi and his assistants always strove for improvements. In February 1902, Poldhu successfully sent experimental messages over 1,152 miles to the American ss. *Philadelphia*, and recognisable signals up to 2,099 miles. Another discovery was made during these tests – radio signals could be transmitted much further by night than by day.

A radio message is transmitted 2,170 miles

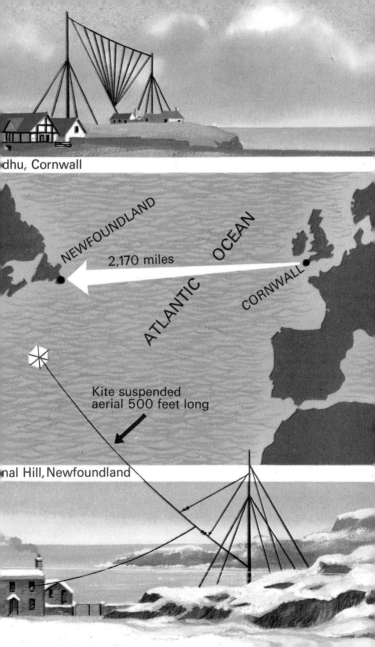

dhu, Cornwall

NEWFOUNDLAND

ATLANTIC OCEAN

2,170 miles

CORNWALL

Kite suspended
aerial 500 feet long

nal Hill, Newfoundland

Marconi's early receivers

The radio receivers Guglielmo Marconi used were indeed strange looking when compared with modern valve or transistorised instruments.

Currents through a coherer caused a small, inked wheel to jiggle up and down over an unwinding paper tape, marking on it the shorts and longs of Morse code messages. Marconi introduced 'tuned' circuits to make his receivers more sensitive and selective, and brought out the famous '7777' patent.

Marconi invented a detector of radio waves called the Magnetic Detector. In this instrument two clockwork-driven ebonite pulleys caused a continuous loop of wire, made up of soft iron strands, to pass through a small glass tube. On this tube were wound a few turns of wire with the ends connected to the aerial-earth circuit. Over the glass tube fitted a bobbin with many more turns of wire wound on it than on the glass tube. The bobbin windings were connected to a pair of head-phones. Two strong horseshoe magnets, with their pole-pieces near to the bobbin, completed the instrument, which changed transmitted radio waves into the dots and dashes of the Morse code.

As the soft iron wire slowly rotated, a magnetic field spread from magnets to wire, but nothing was heard in the headphones until transmitted radio waves induced high-frequency currents into the receiving aerial, and these, passing through the windings on the glass tube, caused the magnetic field to collapse suddenly across the bobbin windings and induce into them currents which became low-pitched signals in the head-phones.

Marconi's detector

MARCONI'S MAGNETIC DETECTOR

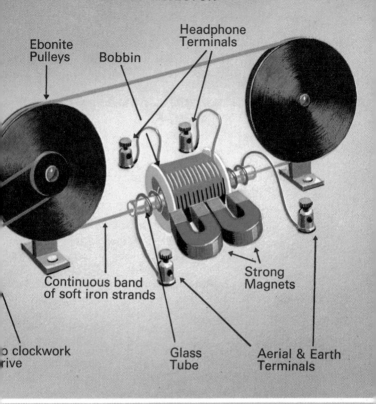

Ebonite Pulleys

Bobbin

Headphone Terminals

Continuous band of soft iron strands

Strong Magnets

Glass Tube

Aerial & Earth Terminals

clockwork drive

MARCONI'S WIRELESS TELEGRAPH

O R S E   C O D E

essage received and decoded on paper tape

Other detectors of radio waves
and Fleming's wonderful invention

Interest in radio was now widespread, and various new detectors of radio waves were discovered.

It was found that crystals such as iron pyrites, molybdenite and carborundum, when contacted by a pinpoint, and combinations like zincite-bornite, could detect radio waves.

There was also the electrolytic detector, which had two electrodes, one of them a fine, sharply-pointed piece of wire, both in water with a drop of sulphuric acid added. All these detectors changed the high-frequency radio currents into audio-frequency currents which gave readable signals.

In 1903, Sir Ambrose Fleming invented the two-electrode valve. This was an electric lamp with a filament, and a second electrode called the 'plate' or 'anode'.

The 'plate' was a flat, thin piece of metal rigidly fixed inside the glass bulb of the lamp. When the filament was heated by an electric current, it shot out clouds of electrons at terrific speed. Electrons are invisible particles of *negatively* charged electricity, and these would only go to the 'plate' when the plate had a *positive* electrical charge. The Fleming valve changed high-frequency radio currents (to which the headphones could not respond) into low-frequency currents which caused signals to be heard in the headphones. Fleming used his valve as a detector of radio waves. It was a wonderful invention, but greater advances were yet to be made.

Diagram of a simple two-electrode valve, showing electrons moving from the filament to the anode

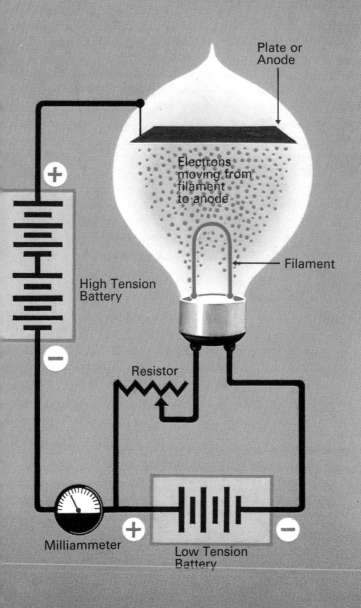

Plate or
Anode

Electrons
moving from
filament
to anode

Filament

High Tension
Battery

Resistor

Milliammeter

Low Tension
Battery

The great discovery of Lee de Forest

Just before Christmas, 1906, a ship's radio officers were astonished to hear, in their headphones, something like violin music and a voice saying, 'If anyone hears me, please write to Mr. Fessenden at Brant Rock'. Fessenden had succeeded in broadcasting his voice and music twenty years before broadcasting for entertainment was begun.

In 1907, Lee de Forest, an American, added to Fleming's two-electrode valve (or diode) a third electrode called a 'grid', and so made the first three-electrode valve, or 'triode'. The 'grid' was sometimes a perforated cylinder of thin metal, or a spiral of fine wire. The 'grid' was rigidly fixed between filament and 'plate'.

Immediately a grid was added to the two-electrode valve, all sorts of things could be done which were not previously possible. The three-electrode valve helped to detect radio waves *and* amplify them – that is, make them much stronger. The triode could be made to *oscillate*, and so help generate radio-frequency waves. Radio communication became much easier, and far more reliable.

Years later, valves containing several electrodes – pentodes, heptodes, etc., in fact two or three valves all working in one glass bulb, were developed.

A ship's officers hear a voice and music on their radio

The Post Office takes over the
main radio stations in Britain

In 1909 the Post Office took over the main radio stations in Britain. Much credit must go to the engineers of the Post Office Research Department for their very valuable work in the development of radio. The Post Office is not allowed to publicise its achievements, but it has been responsible for a great deal of progress in radio theory, design and practice.

In 1909, British Post Office radio stations were in touch with only a few hundred vessels. Today they are in radio contact with about 10,000 ships, many of which are at far distant parts of the world. Post Office radio stations handle about 850,000 messages and 150,000 radio-telephone calls every year. This traffic is rapidly increasing.

In 1926 began the first long-distance radio telephone service from the high-powered Post Office radio station at Rugby, to places 2,800 miles away in America.

Sir William Preece, K.C.B., F.R.S., died in 1913. He had been chief-engineer to the Post Office, and had greatly advanced the science of radio as a result of his great work at the Post Office and his encouragement of the young Marconi. Before he died, he saw the entire world linked by radio.

A modern Post Office radio tower

The first use of radio to bring a criminal to justice

The year was 1910. A Doctor Crippen was wanted by Scotland Yard for the murder of his wife. Crippen tried to escape the law by sailing for Halifax, Nova Scotia, on the liner *Montrose*. With him, dressed as a young man, went his secretary, Miss Le Neve.

Crippen thought he had got safely away, but Captain Kendall of the *Montrose* became suspicious of these two passengers and sent a radio message to England, saying that Doctor Crippen was on board.

Inspector Dew of Scotland Yard at once sailed in the White Star liner *Laurentic*, which was a good deal faster than the *Montrose*, and arrived first at Halifax. When the *Montrose* arrived at Halifax, Inspector Dew boarded her, arrested Crippen and took him back to England for trial.

In 1911, in Italy, a man stole 300,000 lire and was making his escape to South America in the liner *Principe Umberto*. Radio telegraphy played a leading part in closing the net around this criminal and he was arrested when the liner arrived at Buenos Aires.

Since those days, radio has often been used to bring evil-doers to justice.

A policeman uses a modern portable transmitter/receiver to report a criminal's movements to headquarters

Heroism of radio officers

Many radio officers have performed brave actions since radio was first fitted in ships.

When the ss. *Volturno* was ablaze in an Atlantic storm, her radio officer stuck to his post continuously for twenty-six hours, sending the morse letters 'CQD' – which was then the distress call. His bravery was responsible for saving the lives of five hundred and twenty passengers and crew.

When the liner *Titanic*'s side was ripped open by an iceberg, her senior radio officer, John George (Jack) Phillips, continuously sent the letters 'CQD' and the newly-agreed letters 'SOS' until, with other ships, the liner *Olympic* was racing to help. Bow down, foredeck awash, the *Titanic* was sinking. Captain Smith told the radio officers to save themselves, but Jack Phillips stayed at his radio until he went down with the ship.

Jack Phillips started the '*Titanic* tradition' which says that as long as the radio instruments work, the radio officer will stick to his post, even to going down with his ship. Many radio officers, in peace-time and during two wars, have upheld the *Titanic* tradition. Hardwick of the P. & O. liner *Egypt*, and O'Loughlin of the liner *Vestris*, are only two of many other very brave men.

If you are at Godalming, do go to see the beautiful memorial to Radio Officer Jack Phillips of the *Titanic*. This memorial is close to Godalming parish church.

As his ship sinks, the radio officer stays at his post

Short waves and the radio amateur

In the early days of radio, it was thought that only long-wave radio transmissions could travel long distances, and so radio amateurs – known as 'hams' – were allowed to broadcast short-wave transmissions. However, to the amazement of the professionals, it was found that short-wave transmissions could be received over long distances.

The usefulness of short waves became known just in time. Britain was on the point of building a chain of enormously expensive long-wave Empire radio stations. This plan was scrapped and instead, a system of short-wave stations was installed throughout the British Empire. They have proved to be marvellously efficient. Many millions of pounds were saved because of the much lower cost of short-wave radio stations.

To radio 'hams' goes the credit of quite a number of clever and useful inventions. Often, when the usual means of communication have broken down in emergencies caused by earthquake, flood, fire and hurricane, radio 'hams' have taken over and, by means of their small, self-built, short-wave radio stations, have helped to arrange rescue operations, the transport of medical and food supplies and the housing of the homeless.

A radio amateur and his equipment

Radio direction finding

Just before 1914, it was discovered that if several turns of wire were wound on a square or round 'former', the 'frame-aerial' thus made acted very differently from the long wire aerial (stretched between high poles) which was the usual sort of radio aerial in the early days of broadcasting and which received signals equally well from any direction. It was found that turning a frame-aerial so that its windings were at right-angles to the direction from which radio waves were coming, reduced the induced signals in the frame-aerial to a minimum strength. If the frame-aerial were pointed directly at the source of transmission, the signals induced in it were much stronger. Try this with your transistor set. As you rotate the receiver, the strength of voice or music varies.

This *directional* property of frame-aerials is now used in 'direction-finders' aboard ships and aircraft. All over the world, on islands, along coastlines and on lightships, radio transmitters send out Morse code letters to identify themselves and their position. By means of directional aerials and a radio receiver – 'D/F' as it is known – an aircraft or a ship can accurately fix its own position in clear weather or fog with the help of these radio signals. The position of other ships or aircraft can also be fixed. Strandings and collisions are thus avoided.

Diagram of the principle of a directional aerial

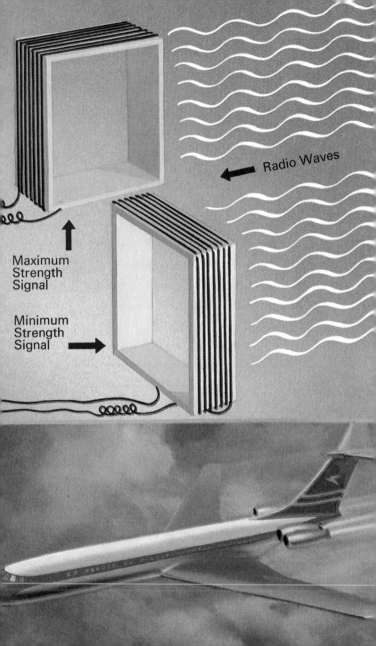

Radio Waves

Maximum
Strength
Signal

Minimum
Strength
Signal

Echoes

No doubt you have often shouted 'Hallo' towards a cliff face or high building, and in a second or two heard the echo – 'Hallo'. When you shouted 'Hallo', the vocal chords in your throat set up sound waves in the air. They travelled at 1,100 feet per second to the cliff face, bounced off it and returned to you.

If, from the time when you shouted 'Hallo', one second passed before you heard the echo, you would know that the distance between you and the cliff face was 550 feet, because sound waves, travelling at 1,100 feet per second, need one second to travel 550 feet to the cliff face and bounce back 550 feet to you.

A ship's echo-meter creates a very high-pitched 'tonk-tonk-tonk' which causes *sound* waves to travel from the ship's bottom through the water to the ocean bed. They then bounce back to the ship's bottom, and are received and recorded with special radio equipment. Because the speed of sound travelling through water is known, the depth of the water can be calculated from the time taken by the sound waves to travel to the ocean bed and back again.

The principle of receiving 'echoes' was later applied to radio waves, and another great step forward was taken in the story of radio.

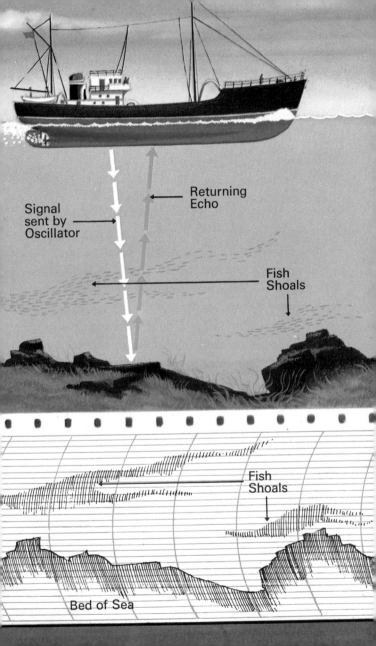

Returning Echo

Signal sent by Oscillator

Fish Shoals

Fish Shoals

Bed of Sea

Radio echoes. Radar – how it works

Not long before 1939, a man in England noticed strange echoes on his radio receiver whenever aircraft passed over. He wondered about these – and invented the first radar set.

Radar is possible because radio waves – which travel at 186,000 miles a second – can also be reflected just like sound or light waves.

A 'scanner', which is attached to a mast and turns round and round, transmits high-frequency radio waves focussed in a narrow beam. (James Clerk Maxwell foretold, a hundred years ago, that radio waves could be focused). Whenever these radio waves strike against a coastline, other ships, aircraft or even rain clouds, they are reflected back to the ship, aircraft or land station that sends out the radio waves from its scanner.

The reflected waves – echoes as they are called – are received by a radar set and show up as glowing spots on a radar screen, which is something like a television screen, making a 'trace' of coastlines, islands, other ships, buoys and any aircraft which are in range.

A 'picture' is, therefore, shown of everything in range of the transmitting radar scanner, and the distance easily calculated. By means of radar, a navigator of a ship or aircraft can accurately fix its position, and avoid any dangers.

A radar screen

A ship in poor visibility and, below, its radar screen

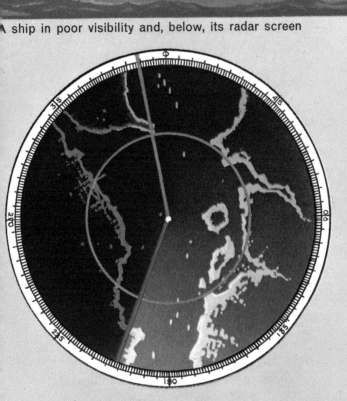

The white spot in the screen's centre indicates the position of the ship using radar. The red line or 'trace' sweeps clockwise around the radar screen leaving a glowing map behind it. The circular purple line is the range marker and can be moved outwards from the centre of the screen when it cuts any part of the 'trace' — ship — headland etc:— its range from the ship reads off on a dial. The blue line reads off its bearing.

Conclusion

Many are the uses of Radio. Ships use radar as their eyes in clear weather or in fog, and use D/F – Direction Finding – for fixing their positions. Weather reports, navigation warnings, time signals, medical advice and news are all sent by radio.

In fog, aeroplanes are 'homed' onto runways by radio, and in Britain they can now be automatically landed by radio control.

The Royal Navy, Army and Royal Air Force use 'walkie-talkies' – small transmitters and receivers. So do the police whose cars are radio fitted, as are ambulances and many taxi-cabs.

Missiles, rockets and satellites are guided by radio. Satellites transmit to Earth, over vast distances, information about outer space, the moon and distant planets. T.V and sound programmes and radio-telephone conversations are relayed by satellites *Telstar* and *Early Bird*.

Britain's wonderful radio-telescope at Jodrell Bank, probes outer space and also tracks satellites.

The story of radio goes on from one exciting chapter to ever more amazing ones. Only a hundred years have passed since that story began. One wonders what new marvels are yet to come.

A modern radio-telescope

THE MORSE CODE

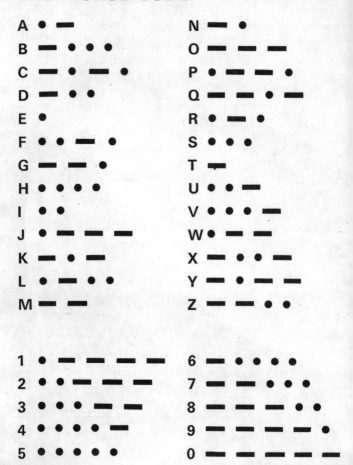

In length of signal a dash is equivalent to three dots.

The Morse Code was invented by an American,
S. F. B. Morse, who lived from 1791 to 1872. It is
used for sending messages by radio, landline
and underwater cables.